The Shalford Book of 20th Century Russian Poetry

Translated by
Richard McKane
with a preface
by Peter Levi,
Oxford Professor of Poetry

Kozmik Press
London   Dallas   Sydney

For my daughter
Juliet

The Shalford Book of 20th Century
Russian Poetry. First published
by Kozmik Press 1985

Translation © Richard McKane
Introduction © Peter Levi

British Library Cataloguing in Publication Data

The Shalford book of 20th century Russian poetry.
  1. Russian poetry—20th century—Translations
  into English   2. English poetry—Translations
  from Russian
  I. McKane, Richard
  891.71′42′08   PG3237.E5

ISBN 0–905116–12–7

Contents

Acknowledgements

Some of the poems in this anthology have been printed before in *OMPHALOS, A MEDITERRANEAN REVIEW* Ed. Peter Mackridge, out of circulation. *NEW DEPARTURES* Ed. Michael Horovitz. *PENGUIN POST WAR RUSSIAN POETRY* Ed. Daniel Weissbort 1973. *SELECTED POEMS OF ANNA AKHMATOVA*. Penguin Books and Oxford University Press 1969. Richard McKane (out of print). *GNOSIS: A RUSSIAN ENGLISH JOURNAL*. NEW YORK Ed. Arkady Rovner and Victoria Andreyeva, *GNOSIS ANTHOLOGY OF CONTEMPORARY AMERICAN AND RUSSIAN LITERATURE AND ART* Ed. Arkady Rovner, Victoria Andreyeva, E. Daniel Richie, Stephen Sartarelli, Gnosis Press, New York.

It has been a privilege to publish my translations in these magazines and anthologies. It is difficult to know which editor has been more supportive. Daniel Weissbort published an authoritative collection of Russian Poetry in Penguin's *Post War Russian Poetry* and it is to there that people should look to plug some of my gaps. Daniel Weissbort also printed several of my Turkish translations in *Modern Poetry in Translation* and translations of the Danish poet Henrik Nordbrandt, who was one of the soundest critics of my own poetry and translations when we were both living in Turkey in the seventies. Nikos Stangos, the poet and translator of Ritsos, who edited *Selected Poems of Anna Akhmatova* for Penguin Books helped me launch my translating career. Arkady Rovner and Victoria Andreyeva have given me all my knowledge of the Russian 'Third Literature'. I closely collaborated with them on my translations of Aranzon, Bokstein and Volokhonsky. It was also an honour that Victoria Andreyeva should translate several of my poems into Russian, simultaneously to my translating her into English. When I was Hodder Fellow in the Humanities at Princeton University from 1978-1979 I got to know Arkady and Victoria better. This book wouldn't have come into being without them or the opportunity that that Fellowship Year gave me. While at Princeton I met Stephen Berg who at that very time was reworking my translations of Anna Akhmatova into his book '*With Akhmatova at the Black Gates.*' Stephen Berg edits the *American Poetry Review*, and was to become a firm friend. He introduced me to my wife-to-be Elizabeth. That year in Princeton many of the Aranzon poems were translated with her in mind, and we collaborated on a translation of

Osip Mandelstam's *Moscow Notebooks* which is still looking for a publisher. I felt a tenderness that year, for Elizabeth, for the world around me, and somehow Aranzon expressed even better than I could except for a few original poems. My thanks to the Faculty of the Humanities at Princeton for awarding me the Fellowship, and my deeper thanks to Elizabeth for making that the best year of my life. Finally Michael Horovitz. We had met once before at Penguin before he got in touch about translating Voznesensky for *New Departures*. He was exceedingly rattled by the security at the Turkish Consulate where I was working at the time, but managed to get up to my desk. We then proceeded to work on the drafts of *Applefall*. It was like ointment being slapped on a sore spot. Collaboration on a translation is one of the most difficult things, but I came to admire Michael's deft parries at the text.

To all these editors and other friends mentioned in these acknowledgements, thanks and this book's for you.

Preface

By Peter Levi, Oxford Professor of Poetry

Between 1833, when Pushkin had finished Onegin and the Bronze Horseman, and 1953, when Pasternak had entered his last phase as a poet, Russian poetry towered and flourished like a tree. In the same period French poetry, an entire countryside of lakes and rivers and waterfalls in the thirties and forties of the last century, has sunk to a few murmuring streams, and English poetry has lived like a gambler through a series of hectic and unlikely successes, but now it has come on times, as everyone knew it would by 1953. Nothing in European poetry, and nothing in the modern history of Europe, is as interesting as Russian poetry. If Tolstoy had been English, what a terrible writer he might have been. If Tennyson had been Russian, as by temperament he almost was, he might have been, I think would have been, a poet as great as Baudelaire.

Still, we must accept things as they are, including politics and history, all our national traditions and our educational malformation. Literature has really no history of its own, but poetry in particular is intricately linked to the history of mankind, and it cannot ever be otherwise. If it seems to represent an attempt to withdraw, to break away or to break out of history, that is because poetry is an inward liberation, truth is the most powerful drug, and a sense of liberation and the breaking of taboos is a vital element in literature. Russian poetry has all of this because it is deadly serious, has roots in growth at a level which is intellectual, aesthetic and in a way spiritual, and is based on human experience of extraordinary tension and calibre. It is much more grown up than the romantic revolution. Maybe it is so modern that we have not quite caught up with it.

Richard McKane is a wonderful poet who has devoted a lifetime to Russian poetry and the art of translation; so much so that from his earliest work as a boy he has had a special inwardness with Russian poets and has gone on developing it to a point where he attained complete authenticity. He has done the same in other languages as well; his Seferis translation is startling and exact, and his Turkish translations are convincing. But Russian, translated by him into English, is so to speak his native language as a poet. His Akhmatova is well known. Every couple of years something surprising arrives from him, always pure original poetry, perfectly his and perfectly itself. In the past thirty years we have seen many talented writers of verse translation, but none better.

vii

He is conscious enough of the tragic quality of life, and he seeks it out in modern poetry, but with a curious luminous sweetness, which I think precisely echoes modern Russian poets, as in his very first poem in this collection, Blok to Akhmatova (1913). I know from experience and failure how tempting it is and how extremely difficult to translate Blok. I think he has Blok as nearly as Blok can be caught now in credible English. His versions are always credible, always interesting, always draw one inside the poem. His Akhmatova versions are unparalleled, and I think a great advance on his admittedly brilliant early work on that wonderful poet. They have a restrained resonance and an extraordinary personal power. I suppose what the poets in his wide range have in common is their intimacy, their personal quality. You need to be a little quiet to listen to them. They flower in the mind rather slowly, and crisp as they are they are not quite immediate, they need to be reread. In Memory of a Friend (1945) seems to be made of nothing, yet not other poem in any language commemorates that time so well or touches one so deeply.

It is one of the simplest and commonest demands of poetry made by ordinary people that one should feel as if someone has taken one by the hand, perhaps from far away. It is also one of the commonest attempts of amateur poets, and the most seldom successful. Akhmatova, in spite of her utter privacy, accomplishes it, and Richard McKane in his versions precisely conveys it. This is the quality which taken against the background of history makes Russian poetry unbearable. But at the same time it has formal patterns and special rhythms of great power and beauty. Akhmatova certainly has them. But in her greatest poems she goes beyond superficial comment of this kind, she is nothing but towering human spirit. The same can be said of Pasternak.

He belonged within a few years to the same generation as the great American poets of the modern movement. His deepest achievement was his extraordinary mastery of his language, firstly struggling with it and at last by riding it as the river-god rides his native river. His poetry could be knotted like wood or it could flow away like silk. I have the impression that Richard McKane catches his tone as no one else has done. His truth to tone results in a certain English awkwardness, but also in great beauty. This in particular is where one is drawn into the centre of every poem, stanza and phrase. He presents a wide and representative selection of the poems, including the neglected early ones. Pasternak himself was worried about their baroque quality, but it underlies all his achievement. Sophokles said something similar about his early work. But the work of such an artist is a progression, it is something complete, not a series of scattered monuments. I am particularly fond of Three Variants (1917) and Pines

(1941), though the Zhivago poems certainly have the strongest immediate impact, and they are terribly memorable. Among the ascendancy of modern Russian poetry for its purity and clarity and force, its individuality, intimacy and seriousness, Pasternak is supreme, and all but unrivalled in European literature in this century.

But Mandelstam is also a great poet, a year younger than Pasternak although he died earlier. Pasternak liked to write in an uncluttered room without books, in a good light, and maybe that is at least symbolically the reason why he cuts at once to the heart of every subject. Mandelstam was an aesthete, as his prose reveals, and a most interesting one. That may be why he is so translatable, he is all gems and ingots, or to put it otherwise, all phrases and images. Nothing in his poetry (and therefore nothing in these well calculated versions) is as casual as it looks.

> How terrifying for the two of us is this life,
> my largemouthed, comrade wife.
>
> See how our Armenian tobacco crumbles,
> little friend, simple one, cracking nuts for your birthday cake.
>
> One could whistle life through like a starling
> or eat it like a slice of hazelnut cake ...
>
> But we both know that's impossible.

October 1930 Tiflis

Why single out this poem except for its lightness, with a rhythmic impetus as tough as steel? But also for innumerable touches, the crumbling tobacco, the starling, the place and date, the hazelnut cake (one wants to eat it, it is like the poem), and the descending tone of 'little friend, simple one ... your birthday cake'. It is an admirable poem that conveys far more than it appears to say. It pretends nothing. It is perfectly honest. It would pass the tests of Brecht and of minimalist poetry. Thomas Hardy would have admired it, though it is outside the scope of his technique. One wishes he had read it.

Okudzhava was born in 1924 and is new to me personally though he is over sixty. No, that is not quite true; he has two poems in a Soviet anthology of 1967 which I preserve for its curious photographs. One is called The Merry Drummer and both appear in verse translations which accurately convey the most rebarbative aspects of Russian verse to English readers, the thumping metre and the genteel elegance. They would have looked old-fashioned in English in 1910. What a difference in

Richard McKane's translations. Okudzhava's poetry is as light as snowflakes, but it covers the ground deeply and densely as snow does. He knows Villon and has an affinity to Brecht or shows his influence. His nearest English equivalent is Charles Causley. There is the same stabilizing linguistic gravel in his poems. He is an important find.

Voznesensky and Yevtushenko are both well known in English. Indeed they both suffer with the critics for their great popularity. Being in the rare position of having helped to translate Yevtushenko when no one had heard of him, I am convinced of the extremely high quality of his work. They are qualities of life. Over twenty-seven years I have often questioned and reconsidered this opinion, but he is still a poet who speaks to me immediately, and his verse is as memorable as Aragon's or Quasimodo's. He is an astonishing poet, like the sun bursting through mist and glittering on a wet forest. Richard McKane does them both justice. His Voznesensky (helped by the author) has a restraint and an unfacile run to it that is lacking in most translations. I wish there were much more of it. The Yevtushenko poems are also few, but a splendid choice, unknown to me.

Aranzon (1939-70) is quite new to me and a much fuller selection. He is a poet of great formality, sadness and sensuousness: almost as if he had fallen asleep in Paris in 1843 and woken now, and these were his waking dreams. But even his sonnets have the after-echo and the ominous tension of modern poetry at its best. One has the impression of powerful strength of spirit, as if a new and more certain age had dawned. One can detect lessons hammered out from literature, something rare in Russian poetry after the generation of Pasternak, from which he inherits.

> Airy flower, without roots,
> here is the butterfly on my hand,
> look, life is given, what can one do with it?

He is not always so quiet. Spring and love are volcanic explosions in his poetry. He inherits among other things the phenomenon of spring in Russia. At first you think it is an earth-shaking literary inspiration from Yesenin, then you realize it is equally to be found in Tolstoy, in Pasternak, and elsewhere. Then you see that this force is real, it is life. Maybe Russian poetry embodies the Russian spring as Greek tragedy embodies the Greek summer and the Greek light. Ilya Bokstein's poem In Memory of Leonid Aranzon has the same intimacy with natural forces which are so soaked in the human spirit and its experience that they do not seem impersonal.

If joking is permitted, one is tempted to say that the old-fashioned

Russian soul is alive and kicking, but there is nothing old-fashioned in the poetry, it really is like a spring river breaking through the ice. The intimate familiarity with life is the lesson of Pasternak, I suppose. It is thrilling to me that there are Russian poets younger than I am who are so individually excellent, who are such masters of their means, who are fit to be named with Pasternak. Eliot, a poet of equally towering greatness in his own strange way, bequeathed a fall-out of ashes, but Pasternak seems to have founded a genuine renaissance of Russian poetry. The new voices are almost more assured than the older ones, and luckily for us they are recognizable by all the old European standards as good, even as great poets. What I chiefly learnt from this collection is that Russian poetry is unexhausted to this day.

Ilya Bokstein is a religious poet in a sense that is somehow impossible in the west, or too full of pitfalls, because it would be too intellectualized, there would be too much taking of an attitude. Or in a way the corresponding English poet might be Ted Hughes. But one does not need to categorize living poets, particularly those younger than oneself. One must open one's eyes and ears, and expect newness. These translations precisely convey a thrilling newness, a force of life expressed in sharpness of technique, like a water-colour sketch of the great period, when the painters made up their own techniques under pressure of reality, and learnt at the same time from one another. It was all a way of expressing light. These poems, many of them sad or tragic, generate a feeling of optimism and openness, a sense of rebirth. One rarely finds that in one's English contemporaries.

Peter Levi

Introduction

This book is a subjective selection of some of the major figures in Russian 20th Century Poetry. Although there are many gaps I feel it is still a representative selection.

It includes Akhmatova's *Requiem*, Osip Mandelstam's *Poem to the Unknown Soldier* and selections from Pasternak's *Zhivago* poems. These are surely three high points of Russian 20th Century Poetry. In *Requiem* Akhmatova becomes the conscience of the nation. In *Poem to the Unknown Soldier*, Osip Mandelstam, with unerring foresight sees the conflict to come in the Second World War, and even in his lines 'I am something new/from me the world will be bright' is forecasting the 'brighter than a thousand suns' atom bomb. Pasternak's *Zhivago* poems must be the height of Russian religious poetry of this century. But as well as that they are fine love poems; poems about love and writing poetry, as can be seen in *Winter Night*. In all three major poets — Akhmatova, Mandelstam and Pasternak, I have included work from their earlier periods. So we get early love poems of Akhmatova, the poems of Mandelstam with classic motifs and the nature poetry of Pasternak.

Andrei Voznesensky, Yevgeny Yevtushenko and to a lesser extent Bulat Okudzhava are well enough known to readers not to need an introduction. Voznesensky's *Applefall* and *Troubadours and Burghers* emerge out of close collaboration with the author and Michael Horovitz. These poems were originally printed in *New Departures*. I am grateful to Michael Horovitz for his support in the translation of these poems. The artist, whose home Voznesensky visits in *Applefall*, is Picasso.

John Roberts, Director of the Great Britain USSR Society, who taught me Russian at Marlborough College, and whose friendship and knowledge of things Russian are a source of great joy to me, long ago suggested that I translate Yevtushenko's *Yes city and No city*. I think that *Yes city and No city* sums up the dual role that Yevgeny Yevtushenko is fated to play in Russian poetry.

It is worth pointing out that the Bulat Okudzhava poems translated here are in fact songs. Okudzhava's popularity as a balladeer earns him a place in this collection.

Leonid Aranzon died in 1970, aged thirty one. He was a screenwriter for scientific films. He lived in Leningrad. When he died, under mysterious circumstances, he had only published some of his children's poetry. I am indebted to my good Russian friend Arkady Rovner, novelist and Editor of *Gnosis*, a bilingual Russian-English journal published in New York, for bringing Aranzon's poetry to my attention. Aranzon combines a vibrant sexuality with a fine lyric tone. I have attempted in the translations to maintain certain of his rhythms. He read his poems in a sonorous bass, sometimes turning his back away from the audience.

Another two poets who belong with Aranzon are Ilya Bokstein and Henri Volokhonsky. All three poets belong to the 'Third Literature', non-official and non-samizdat/dissident. Let us see what Arkady Rovner and Victoria Andreyeva, Russian Editors of the *Gnosis Anthology of Contemporary American and Russian Literature and Art* say about Ilya Bokstein: 'Bokstein started within a movement of 'schizoid poetry' which was a surrealist challenge to a profane sobriety and literalness; and through meditative and esoteric poetry, he came to the ultimate point of poetic subjectivism — to 'extremist poetry', which utilizes a system of poetic codes, and unites poet and visionary while excluding the possibility of a profane judgement.' Ilya Bokstein was born in 1937 in Moscow. He was imprisoned for his poetry recitation in Mayakovsky Plaza and spent five years (1961-1966) in prison camps in Mordovia. In 1972 he left Russia for Israel.

Henri Volokhonsky was born in Leningrad in 1936, and received his college degree in Limnology. Since 1973 he has lived in Tiberias, Israel, working on a study of Lake Dinaret. He combines a lofty prophetic tone with an intense spirituality. In his poetry the classical style harmonises with the *avant garde*.

Richard McKane
Shalford House, LONDON SE1

ALEXANDER BLOK 1880-1921

To Anna Akhmatova

'Beauty is terrifying.' They'll say to you.
Languidly you throw your
Spanish shawl over your shoulders,
a red rose in your hair.

'Beauty is simple.' They'll say to you,
and you will cover your child
with a check shawl with hands unskilled,
a red rose on the floor.

But you will listen in a haze
to all the words, breaking out around,
and will contemplate sadly
and repeat to yourself about yourself.

'I am not terrifying. I am not simple;
I am not so terrifying to simply
kill, not so simple
that I do not know how terrifying life is.'

    16th December 1913

The Unknown One

In the evenings over the restaurants
the hot air is wild and dull,
and the spring, the decaying spirit,
is governed by the shouts of drunks.

In the distance over the backstreet dust,
over the boredom of the out-of-town summer-houses
the whirl of the croissant turns light gold,
and a child's crying resounds.

And every evening, beyond the barriers,
breaking up the pots and pans
the experienced wits
stroll past the ditches with their ladies.

Rowlocks squeak over the lake,
and a woman's scream resounds,
and in the sky, trained for everything
the moon's disc senselessly warps.

Every evening my only friend
is reflected in my glass,
and is calm and drowned
in the acrid secret liquid.

At the neighbouring tables
the sleepy lackeys stick out,
and drunkards with rabbit eyes
shout 'In vino veritas!'

And every evening at an appointed hour,
(Or do I only dream this?)
a girl's figure, swathed in silks,
moves in the misty window.

And slowly making her way through the drunks,
always without companions, alone,
breathing perfume and mists,
by the window she sits.

Her supple silks
waft ancient superstitions,
and her hat with mourning feathers,
and her slender hand with rings.

Chained by the strange proximity
I look at her dark veil,
and see an enchanted shore
and an enchanted distance.

Dim secrets are extended me,
some sun is promised me,
and all the contortions of my soul
are pierced by the acrid wine.

The drooping ostrich feathers
rock in my brain,
and bottomless blue eyes
flower on the distant shore.

A treasure lies in my soul,
and the key is given only to me!
You're right, drunk monster!
I know, truth is in wine.

       24th April 1906

ANNA AKHMATOVA 1889-1966

Garden

The whole icebound garden
sparkles and crackles.
He who leaves me is sad,
but there is no path back.

And the sun, a pale dull face
is just a round window;
I secretly know whose double
has clung to it for so long.

My calm is for ever taken up
with a premonition of trouble,
yesterday's footprints
still show through the ice.

The dull, dead face leaned down
over the dumb sleep of the fields,
sharp cries of the last
migrating cranes fade.

Ice floes ringingly flow,
the skies are hopelessly pale.
Oh why do you punish me?
I don't understand my guilt.

Kill me if necessary,
but don't be hard on me.
You don't want children from me
and you don't like my poems.

Have it your way then,
I kept my oath.
I gave you my life — but this sadness
I take with me to the grave.

This meeting has been sung by no one,
and without songs sadness has died down.
Cool summer has come,
like the beginning of new life.

The sky seemed to be a stone dome,
poison-tinged with yellow fire.
More than my daily bread
I craved one word, one word about him.

Enliven my soul with some news,
like the dew sprinkling the grass,
not for passion or for pleasure,
but for the sum of the world's love.

1916 Slepnevo

You thought that I too was the type
that you could forget,
and that I'd throw myself pleading and weeping
under the hooves of a bay mare,

or that I'd ask the sorcerers
for some magic potion made from roots
and send you a terrible gift:
my precious perfumed handkerchief.

Then be accursed. I will not touch
your damned soul with a groan or a glance.
But I swear to you by the garden of the angels,
I swear by the miracle-working ikon,
and by the fire and smoke of our nights:
I will never return.

    July 1921

The Muse

In the night when I wait for her to come
life seems to hang on a hair strand.
What are honours, what is youth, what is freedom
before the dear guest with the little pipe in her hand?

There, she has entered. She threw back her shawl,
and looked at me attentively.
I ask her: 'Was it you who dictated
to Dante the pages of Inferno?' She answers: 'It was I.'

     1924

       *   *   *

Here began Pushkin's exile,
and Lermontov's exile ended.
Here the fragrant mountain grasses bend,
and only once did I succeed in seeing while
by the lake under the deep shade of the plane tree
in that cruel hour before evening
the unslaked eyes shining
of the immortal lover of Tamara.

     Kislovodsk 1927

Slander

Everywhere slander accompanied me.
It's crawling pace I heard in my sleep,
and in the dead town under a merciless sky,
straying at random behind roof and cornfield.
Its reflection burned in all eyes,
now as betrayal, now as innocent terror,
I don't fear it. At every new challenge
I have a worthy and stern reply.
But I already forsee an inescapable day:
my friends will come to me at dawn
and trouble my sweetest sleep with sobbing,
and place an ikon on my chilled chest.
Unknown to anyone it will enter then.
In my blood its insatiable mouth will
not tire of counting non-existent offences,
weaving its voice in the praying of the requiem,
and its shameful delirium will be grasped by all,
so that neighbour cannot look at neighbour,
so that my body will remain in terrible emptiness,
so that for the last time my soul will burn
with earthly weakness, flying in the dawn haze,
and burn with wild pity for the earth it has left.

Boris Pasternak

He who compared himself to a horse's eye,
squints, looks, sees, recognises,
and already the puddles shine
in a diamond fusion, the ice pines away.

The backyards rest in a lilac haze,
platforms, logs, leaves, clouds,
the engine's whistles, the crunch of melon peel,
a timid hand in a fragrant kid glove.

He rings, thunders, gnashes, beats in the breakers —
and is suddenly quiet, this means
he is treading the pine needles, fearful lest
he should scare awake the light dream-sleep of space.

And this means that he is counting the grains
in the empty ears, this means
he has come again from some funeral
to the cursed, black, Daryal tombstones.

Moscow tedium burns again,
death's sleigh bells ring in the distance —
Who has got lost two steps from home,
where the snow is waist deep and an end to all?

Because he compared smoke with the Laocoon,
sang of the graveyard thistle,
because he filled the earth with a new sound
in a new space of mirrored stanzas,

he is rewarded with a form of eternal childhood,
with the bounty and vigilance of the stars,
the whole world was his inheritance
and he shared it with everyone.

19th January 1936

Voronezh

O.M.

The town stands completely icebound.
Trees, walls, snow as though under glass.
Timidly I walk over the crystals.
Uncertain run of the patterned sledge.
Crows over St. Peter's in Voronezh,
and poplars and the bright green sky vault,
eroded, turbid in the sun dust,
and the slopes wave with the Kulikovo battle
of the powerful victorious earth.
The poplars like clashed cups
suddenly ring out over us more powerfully,
like one thousand guests drinking
to our triumph at a wedding feast.

In the room of the exiled poet
fear and the Muse stand duty in turn.
And the night moves on
that knows no dawn.

    1936

Dante

Il mio bel San Giovanni
Inferno. Dante.

He didn't return to his old city,
Florence, even after his death.
That other did not look back as he went away,
and I sing my song to him.
The torch, the night, the final embrace,
the wild shriek of fate by the threshold.
He sent a curse on her from Hell,
and could not forget her in Heaven,
but barefoot, in a sinner's shirt,
with a lit candle he did not walk
through his beloved Florence,
faith-smashed, low, long-awaited.

    1936

Let's celebrate our last anniversary.
Remember that on this day exactly,
the snowy night of our first — diamond —
winter is being repeated again.

Steam rises from the Tsarskoe stables,
the Moika is drowned in darkness,
the light of the moon seems to be extinguished on purpose
and where we're going I cannot tell.

The tousled garden got lost
among the graves of the grandson and the grandfather.
The street lamps burn funereally,
diving out of a prison delirium.

The Field of Mars menaces with icebergs,
and the Lebyazhaya Canal is crystal lain,
what fate can you compare with mine,
when joy and fear are in the soul?

And your voice like a miraculous bird
trembles over my shoulder.
The snow dust is silvered so warmly,
fired by the sudden rays of the sun.

     1938

Dedication on a Book

To M.L. Lozinsky

From a shade almost beyond the Lethe,
in the hour when worlds are being destroyed,
take this gift of spring
in answer to your own best gifts,
so that that high freedom of the soul,
uncrushable and true,
above all times of the year,
fated in friendship
may smile to me as tenderly
as thirty years ago ...
The fence in the Summer Garden
and snowbound Leningrad
arose as in this book
from the magic mirror's haze
and over the Lethe, lost in thought,
the shepherd's reed pipe came to life and played.

    May 1940

Mayakovsky in 1913

I didn't know you when you were famous,
I only remember your stormy dawn,
but perhaps it's right today to dwell on
those distant years' days.
The sounds gathering strength in your poems,
the new voices whirling in . . .
Your young hands did not know the word laziness,
and you reared menacing forests.
Everything you touched seemed transformed
from what it had been before.
What you destroyed, was utterly destroyed,
and its death sentence rang in every sentence.
Not content with a twilight life
you accelerated your fate through impatience,
knowing that you would soon emerge
happy and free for the great struggle.
And already the answering rumble and roar of the tides' wash
was audible in your readings to us,
the rain slanted its eyes crossly,
you argued headlong with the city.
And an as yet unheard of name flashed
like lightning into the choking atmosphere of the hall,
so as now, honoured throughout the country,
to explode like a Very flare.

1940

21

In Memory of a Friend

And on Victory day, tender, misty,
when the dawn as the sunset is red,
spring, late in coming, is fussy,
like a widow by a nameless grave bed.
She doesn't hurry to get off her knees, kneels down
on the soil and strokes the rough grass,
and sets a butterfly from her shoulder onto the ground,
and the first dandelion's down clock puffs past.

　　1945

The Death of the Poet

Yesterday an unrepeatable voice fell silent,
and the converser with the forests went away.
He turned into the life-giving ear of corn,
or the fine rain that he sang of.
And all the flowers that ever flowered in the world
burst into blossom to meet his death.
But suddenly a silence fell
on the planet with the humble name ... earth.

1960

23

Our Own Land

There is no people more proud, more
simple than us.   1922

We don't wear it in sacred amulets on our chests.
We don't compose hysterical poems about it.
It does not delineate our bitter dream-sleep.
It doesn't seem to be the promised land.
We don't make out of it a soul
object for sale and barter,
and we sick, lame, poverty-stricken do not hover above it,
we don't even record memories of it.
But for us it's mud on the boots,
     for us it's crunch on the teeth
     and we mill mess and crush
     that mingled dust and ash.
But we'll lie in it and be in it,
that's why in that song of freedom we call it our own.

     1961 Leningrad

Komarovo Jottings

O, Muse of Crying …
M. Tsvetayeva

… And here I retired from everything,
from every earthly blessing.
The forest tree snag root
became the spirit — the preserver of this place.

In life we are all in a way guests,
living is only a habit,
and I hear on the aerial roads
two voices calling each other.

Two? And still by an Eastern wall,
in the undergrowth of the raspberries,
the dark fresh branch of an elderberry tree …
That is a letter from Marina.*

> 1961 November
> in Gavan' Leningrad
> (in delirium)

* Marina Tsvetayeva, who hanged herself in 1940, wrote a poem dated 11th September 1931 — 21st May 1935 titled 'Buzina': Elderberry.

The Last Rose

You write about us glancing sidelong,
J. Brodsky

I should kneel to pray with the Morozovaya,
dance with Herod's murderess daughter,
fly in smoke from Dido's pyre,
to be with Joan on *her* funeral pyre.
Oh Christ! Don't you see I'm tired
of resurrecting, dying and living.
Take everything, just leave me the feeling
of the freshness of this crimson rose.

Komarovo 1962

Hearthwarming

To E.S. Bulgakova

1. The Mistress

In this room a witch
lived before me.
Her shadow can still be seen
on the eve of the new moon.
Her shadow still stands
by the high threshold,
and evasively and sternly
looks at me.
I myself am not one of those
who is under the power of other charms,
I myself ... But, however, I will not
give away my secrets for nothing.

1943

2. Guests

'... You are drunk,
and all the same it's time to go ...'
Don Juan grown old
and Faust grown young again
bumped into each other by my door —
from the bar and from a meeting!
Or was this only the rocking of twigs
under a black wind,
with the green magic of beams
poured like poison, and yet —
they are like two people known to me,
so alike that one feels revulsion.

1943

3. Treachery

Not because the mirror shattered,
not because the wind whined in the chimney pipe,
not because in thought of you already
something seeped through,
not because, definitely not because
I met him on the threshold.

1944

4. Meeting

Like the happy refrain
of a terrible little song —
he goes along the shaky staircase
having overcome parting.
Not I to him, but he to me —
and doves in the window ...
And the courtyard in ivy, and you in a cloak
according to my word.
Not him to me, but I to him,
    in the darkness,
        in the darkness,
            in the darkness.

Tashkent 1943

In 1940

1

When they bury the epoch,
they sing no funeral incantation.
The nettles, thistles and the dock
will cling as its only decoration.
And only the gravediggers work,
for that cannot wait,
and it's so still, my God so still,
that one can hear time's slow gait.
Then the epoch flows out
like a corpse in a river in spring,
and the son will fall out with his mother
and the grandchild will turn away crying,
and heads are hanging
lower and the moon proceeds with a pendulum swing.
And this, this is the stillness
over fallen Paris.

2
To The Londoners

Time is writing Shakespeare's twenty fourth drama,
with a hand passionless and clear,
and we, the participants of this terrible orgy
better read Hamlet, Caesar or King Lear
by the molten lead river.
Better now to accompany Juliet
to the grave with torch and singing,
better to look through the window at Macbeth
and tremble with the hired murderer,
but not this, not this, not this,
this even we aren't capable of reading.

3
Shadow
What does one woman know about the hour of death.
O. Mandelstam.
You, always more elegant, more tall than all of them, more like a rose,
why do you float up from the bottom of that dead age,
and before my predatory memory arose
your clear profile through the glass of the carriage.
Do you remember the arguments of whether you were a bird or an angel?
The poet called you straw girl.
The tender light of your Georgian eyes
looked the same through their black eyelashes at the whole world.
O shadow! Forgive me, but sleeplessness,
Flaubert, clear weather and the late lilac
reminded me of you, the beauty of 1913, and brought back
that day cloudless and passionless,
and, shadow, memories of this order
throw my mind into disorder.

4

Didn't I know sleeplessness'
every pit and chasm?
But this is like the thunder of cavalry horses
under the wild trumpet blast.
I go into the deserted houses,
into where someone lived once,
all is quiet in the rooms,
only white shadows swim in the mirror's trance.
What's there in the mist's fusion,
Denmark or Normandy — wait —
have I been here in another reincarnation,
and is this a transcription
of those eternally forgotten minutes?

But I warn you, this time
I am living for the last time.
Not as a swallow, not as a cedar,
not as a reed or a star,
not as the spring water,
not as the bell tower chimes,
will I disturb anyone
and with a hopeless groan
visit others' dreams.

The Secrets of the Craft

1. Creation

This is how it happens: a sort of languor;
clocks strike incessantly in my ears;
in the distance the crashing of dying down thunder.
The groans and complaints of unknown,
of imprisoned voices come to me,
some secret ring is tightening,
but from the abyss of whispers and chimes,
one sound arises that conquers them all.
And round it all is incorrigibly still,
then one can hear the grass growing in the forest,
and skipping along the ground with a little basket.
And now words can be heard,
and the little signal chimes of light rhymes,
and then I begin to understand
and the poems simply dictated
lie in the snowwhite notebook.

1936

2.

Arrays of odes mean nothing to me,
or the chimes of elegiac endeavours.
I think in poems all should be out of place,
and not the way it is in life.

If you only knew from what rubbish
poems grow, not knowing shame,
like a yellow dandelion by the fence,
like burdocks and goose grass.

An angry shout, the fresh smell of tar,
mysterious mold on a wall . . .
and already the poem resounds, full of life, tender,
for my delight and yours.

1940

3. The Muse

How can I live with this burden
which they still call the Muse?
People say: 'You're with her on the meadow ...'
People say: 'The babbling of the Gods ...'
Crueller than a recurrent fever back it quivers,
then there's a whole year without a mutter or a murmur.

4. The Poet

If you think about it, this carefree
life is still hard work.
To eavesdrop on music
and jokingly give it out as your own.

And when you've put into a poem
some happy scherzo,
to swear that your poor heart
is groaning with pain among the sparkling crops.

And then to eavesdrop on the forest,
on the pines which appear vowed to silence,
when the smoky veil
of the mist hangs all around.

I take from the right, I take from the left,
and even without any guilty feelings,
a little from crafty life,
and all from the stillness of night.

> 1959, Summer
> Komarovo

5. The Reader

You mustn't be particularly unhappy,
and above all not cryptic. Oh no!
The poet is wide open
so as to make himself clear to the modern man.

And the ramp buckles under the legs,
everything dead, void, bright,
the brow branded by the cold
flame of the lime light.

And each reader is like a secret,
like a treasure trove buried deep in the earth,
the ultimate one, the chance one,
silent throughout life from birth.

There is everything there that nature will ever hide
from us, when it suits her whim,
there someone cries hopelessly
at some appointed hour,

and how dark the night is there,
and the shadow, and how cool it is,
there unknown eyes
talk with me till dawn.

On some things they rebuke me,
on others they agree with me,
so the mute confession flows on,
heat generated from a hallowed conversation.

Our life runs fast on this earth,
and the appointed circle is tight,
and he is incorruptible, eternal,
the unknown friend of the poet.

> 1959, Summer
> Komarovo

6. Last Poem

One poem, as though disturbed by the thunder,
bursts into my home with a breath of life,
laughs, vibrates in the throat,
circles and applauds.

Another poem, born of the midnight stillness,
comes to me from I know not where,
looks for the empty mirror
and mutters to me sternly.

And there are others too, daylight ones,
almost as if they haven't seen me,
that stream onto the white paper
like a clear spring in the valley.

And here's another: a mysterious one that prowls about,
not a sound, not a colour, not a colour, not a sound,
sets boundaries, changes, coils up,
and won't give itself up alive.

But this one! It drank blood drop by drop,
like a wicked young girl drinks love,
and not having said a word to me
it becomes the silence again.

For me this is the cruellest disaster of fate,
it's gone and its tracks lead
to some extreme extreme,
and without it ... I die.

> 1959

7. Epigram

Could Biche compose like Dante,
or Laura glorify the heat of love?
I taught women to speak ...
But, Lord, how can I force them to be quiet?

> (1960)

8. On Poetry
To Vladimir Narbut
It is what I squeezed out of sleepless nights,
it is the bent candles' tallow dimly burning,
it is the first morning chime
of a hundred white bells ...
It is the warm windowsill
under the Chernigov moon,
it is bees, it is a well,
it is dust and mist, and sultry heat.

1940

9.
To Osip Mandelstam
How putrid the smell of a carnation
that I once dreamed of there;
there where Eurydices circle round,
and the bull carried Europa over the waves;
there where our shadows are projected
on the Neva, the Neva, the Neva,
there where the Neva splashes on the steps —
it is your escape route into immortality.

1957

10.
And there are many more things
that cry out to be expressed in my songs:
the wordless that thunders,
and sharpens on subterranean rock in the dark,
or bursts through the smoke.
My account with fire, with wind,
with water is still unsettled,
and that's why my dozings
will suddenly throw wide the door for me,
and proceed under the morning star.

1942

Cinque

Autant que toi sans doute, il
te sera fidèle,
Et constant jusques à la mort.
Baudelaire

1

I remember your words
like on the edge of a cloud,

and from my words for you
the nights became brighter than the days.

So, torn away from the earth,
we walked high as the stars.

Not desperation, not shame,
not now, not after, not then.

But alive and awake
you hear me calling you.

And that door you opened just a little
I have no strength to slam.

26th November 1945

2

Sounds decay in the ether,
and the dawn pretended to be darkness.
In the eternally numbed world,
just two voices: yours and mine.
And under the wind from the invisible Ladoga,
through almost a ringing of bells,
the night conversation was turned
into the light sparkle of crossed rainbows.

20th December 1945

From days long gone by
I have never liked people to pity me,
and I walk on with the drop of your pity
in me like the sun in my body.
That's why the dawn is all around.
I go on working wonders,
that's why!

20th December 1945

4

You know yourself that I will not begin to glorify
that most bitter day of our meeting.
What can remain in your memory,
my shade? What do you want my shade for?
The dedication of a burnt drama,
from which there is no ash,
or a terrible New Year portrait
suddenly coming out of the frame?
Or the chink of birch embers
barely, barely heard,
or that which they did not succeed
in telling me about another's love.

6th January 1946

We didn't breathe in sleepy poppies,
and we don't know our guilt.
Under just what star signs
are we born to bring grief on ourselves?
And what Hell's broth
did this January darkness bring us?
And what invisible glow
forced us out of our minds before light?

11th January 1946

Requiem 1935-1940

No, not under the vault of another sky,
not under the shelter of other wings,
I was with my people then,
there where my people were doomed to be.

1961

Instead of a Foreword
During the terrible years of Yezhovshchina* I spent
seventeen months in the prison queues in Leningrad.
One day someone recognised me. Then a woman with
lips blue with cold who was standing behind me, and of
course had never heard of my name, came out of the
numbness which affected us all and whispered in my
ear — (we all spoke in whispers there):
    'Can you describe this?'
    I said, 'I can!'
    Then something resembling a smile slipped over what
had once been her face.

1 April 1957

* 'Yezhovshchina': Yezhov was head of Stalin's secret police in the late
1930's and was himself purged.

Dedication

The mountains bend before this grief,
the great river does not flow,
but the prison locks are strong,
and behind them the convicts' holes,
and a deathly sadness.
For someone the fresh wind blows,
for someone the sunset basks ...
We don't know, we are the same everywhere;
we only hear the repellent clank of keys,
the heavy steps of the soldiers.
We rose as though to early mass,
and went through the savage capital,
and we used to meet there, more lifeless than the dead,
the sun lower, the Neva mistier,
but in the distance hope still sings.
Condemned ... Immediately the tears start,
one woman, already isolated from everyone else,
as though her life had been wrenched from her heart,
as though she had been smashed flat on her back,
still, she walks on ... staggers ... alone ...
Where now are the chance friends
of my two hellish years?
What do they see in the Siberian blizzard,
what comes to them in the moon's circle?
I send them my farewell greeting.

    March 1940

Introduction

It was a time when only the dead
smiled, happy in their peace.
And Leningrad dangled like a useless pendant
at the side of its prisons.
A time when, tortured out of their minds
the convicted walked in regiments,
and the steam whistles sang
their short parting song.
Stars of death stood over us,
and innocent Russia squirmed*
under the bloody boots,
under the wheels of black Marias.

* 'Russia': In the Russian — 'Rus', the traditional name for Russia

1

They took you away at dawn,
I walked after you as though you were being borne out,
the children were crying in the dark room,
the candle swam by the ikon-stand.
The cold of the ikon on your lips.
Death sweat on your brow ... Do not forget!
I will howl by the Kremlin towers
like the wives of the Streltsy*.

 1935

* 'Like the wives of the Streltsy': the Streltsy were a body of soldiers
organised about 1550 by Ivan the Terrible. Their suppression enabled
Peter I to establish a regular army. In 1698 Peter defeated them outside
Moscow, executed 800 of them and disbanded the others.

2

The quiet Don flows quietly,
the yellow moon goes into the house,

goes in with its cap askew,
the yellow moon sees the shadow.

This woman is sick,
this woman is alone,

husband in the grave, son in prison,
pray for me.

3

No, this is not me — someone else suffers.
I couldn't stand this: let black drapes
cover what happened,
and let them take away the street lights ...
 Night.

If I could show you, the mocker,
everybody's favourite,
happy sinner of Tsarskoe Selo,
how your life will turn out:
you will stand at Kresty*
three hundredth in the line with your prison parcel,
and set fire to the new year ice
with your hot tears.
There the prison poplar sways,
silence — and how many
innocent lives are ending there …

'*Kresty': a prison built on the Vyborg side of Leningrad in 1893. It literally
means 'Crosses' (referring to the layout of the buildings) — and the
additional sense of 'standing before the cross' should be borne in mind; cf.
parts 6 and 10.

For seventeen months I have been screaming,
calling you home.
I flung myself at the executioner's feet.
You are my son and my terror.
Everything is confused for ever,
and I can no longer tell
beast from man,
and how long I must wait for the execution.
Only the dusty flowers,
the clank of censers, and tracks
leading somewhere to nowhere.
An enormous star
looks me straight in the eye
and threatens swift destruction.

    1939

Weightless weeks fly by,
I will never grasp what happened.
How the white nights looked
at you, my son, in prison,
how they look again
with the burning eye of the hawk,
they speak of your tall cross,
they speak of death.

> 1939

Verdict

The stone word fell
on my still living breast.
Never mind, I was prepared,
somehow I'll come to terms with it.

Today I have much work to do:
I must finally kill my memory,
I must, so my soul can turn to stone,
I must learn to live again.

Or else ... The hot summer rustle,
like holiday time outside my window.
I have felt this coming for a long time,
this bright day and the empty house.

> Summer 1939

8
To Death

You will come anyway — so why not now?
I am waiting for you — it's very difficult for me.
I have put out the light and opened the door
to you so simple and wonderful.
Assume any shape you like,
burst in as a poison gas shell,
or creep up like a burglar with a heavy weight,
or poison me with typhus vapours.
Or come with a denunciation thought up by you
and known *ad nauseam* to everyone,
so that I may see over the blue cap*
the janitor's fear-whitened face.
I don't care now. The Yenisey rolls on,**
the Pole star shines.
And the blue lustre of loving eyes
conceals the final horror.

     19 August 1939

* 'the blue cap' and 'the janitor': an arrest.
** 'Yenisey': river in Siberia where many of the
concentration camps were.

9

Already madness has covered
half my soul with its wing,
and gives me strong liquor to drink,
and lures me to the black valley.

I realized that I must
hand victory to it,
as I listened to my delirium,
already alien to me.

It will not allow me to take
anything away with me,
(however I beseech it,
however I pester it with prayer):

not the terrible eyes of my son,
the rock-like suffering,
not the day when the storm came,
not the prison visiting hour,

nor the sweet coolness of hands,
nor the uproar of the lime trees' shadows,
nor the distant light sound —
the comfort of last words.

4 May 1940

10
Crucifixion

'Weep not for Me, Mother,
I am in the grave.'

1

The choir of angels glorified the great hour,
the heavens melted in flames.
He said to His Father: 'Why hast thou forsaken Me?'
and to His Mother: 'Oh, weep not for Me ...'

2

Mary Magdalene smote her breast and wept,
the disciple whom He loved turned to stone,
but where the Mother stood in silence
nobody even dared look.

1940-1943

Epilogue

1

I found out how faces droop,
how terror looks out from under the eyelids,
how suffering carves on cheeks
hard pages of cuneiform,
how curls ash-blonde and black
turn silver overnight,
a smile fades on submissive lips,
fear trembles in a dry laugh.
I pray not for myself alone,
but for everyone who stood with me,
in the cruel cold, in the July heat,
under the blind, red wall.

2

The hour of remembrance has drawn close again.
I see you, hear you, feel you.

The one they hardly dragged to the window,
the one who no longer treads this earth,

the one who shook her beautiful head,
and said: 'Coming here is like coming home.'

I would like to call them all by name,
but the list was taken away and I cannot tell.

For them I have woven a wide shroud
from the humble words I heard among them.

I remember them always, everywhere,
I will never forget them, whatever comes.

And if they gag my tormented mouth
with which one hundred million people cry,

then let them also remember me
on the eve of my remembrance day.

47

If they ever think of building
a memorial to me in this country,

I solemnly give my consent,
only with this condition: not to build it

near the sea where I was born:
my last tie with the sea is broken:

nor in Tsarsky Sad by the hallowed stump
where an inconsolable shadow seeks me,

but here, where I stood three hundred hours,
and they never unbolted the door for me.

Since even in blessed death I am terrified
that I will forget the thundering of Black Marias,

forget how the hateful door slammed,
how an old woman howled like a wounded beast.

Let the melting snow stream
like tears from my motionless, bronze eyelids,

let the prison dove call in the distance
and the boats go quietly on the Neva.

      March 1940

BORIS PASTERNAK 1890-1960

Three Variants

1

When the whole day is weighed before us
in its minutest detail,
only the hot rustling of the squirrel
disturbs the resinous forest.

And in a haze, gathering strength drop by drop
sleeps the row of pine crests,
in streams sweat drops,
husked and peeled the forest.

2

The gardens are homesick with the expanse of silence,
the unconsciousness of the furious gorges
is more fearful than the hurricane, fiercer
than the storm, that rinses and rages.

The cloudburst is close. A smell comes
from the dry mouth of nettles,
thatch, decay and fear and in columns
rises the lowing and roar of the cattle.

3

Dispersed clouds break down
and grow on the bushes. In the gardens
the mouth is full of damp nettle down,
this smell of storms and graveyards.

The briar is tired of groaning,
flights flash and multiply in the sky.
In the naked azure advancing
over the marsh, barefoot tracks go by.

They gleam, they gleam like lips
untouched on a girl's face,
the leaves of the oak, the willow slips
and hoofprints by the watering place.

St. Petersburg 1917

Pines

In the grass among the wild balsam,
the ox-eye daisies and forest lilies
we are lying, our arms outstretched
and heads thrown back against the sky.

The grass in the pine glade
is thick and impenetrable.
We exchange glances and again
change places and positions.

And so, immortal for a time,
we are numbered among the company of pines
and freed from pains
epidemics and death.

With a measured monotony,
the thick blue sky like ointment
lazes to the ground in sunbeams
and stains our sleeves.

We share in the rest of the pine forest
to the music of swarming insects,
breathe in the pines' sleep inducing
fusion of lemon and incense.

Fiery trunks spring
so violently against the blue sky,
and for so long we leave
our hands under our reclining heads,

and there is such breadth in the view,
and from outside all is so submissive
that somewhere beyond the tree trunks
the sea continually appears to me.

There the waves are higher than these branches
and collapsing off a cliff
they shoot a hail of flaming shrimps
from the turbulent bottom.

And in the evening the sunset
is drawn behind a tug on net floats,
flecks of fish oil
and dull smoky amber.

Night falls, and gradually
the moon buries all traces
under the white magic of foam,
under the black magic of water.

The waves are getting louder and higher,
and the people in the restaurant
crowd round a column with an advertisement
indiscernible in the distance.

    1941

From the Poems of Yuri Zhivago

1
Hamlet

The murmur quietens down. I walk out onto the stage.
Leaning against the door-post,
I catch in a distant echo
what will happen in my century.

The darkness of night is trained on me
by a thousand binoculars.
If it be only possible, Abba, Father,
carry this cup past me.

I love your stern master plan
and agree to play this part.
But now another drama is taking place,
and this time let me be discharged.

The order of acts is forethought,
and the end of the way cannot be turned back.
I am alone. Everything drowns in Pharisaism.
Living life is not crossing a field.

8
The Wind

My end has come, but you are living.
And the wind complaining and crying
rocks the forest and the dacha.
Not each pine separately
but all the trees in unison,
with all the boundless distance,
like the hulks of the sailing boats
on the smooth of the ships' bay.
And this not out of daring
or out of aimless fury
but in my anguish to find the words
for you for a cradle lullaby.

14
August

As it promised without deception
the sun burst through early in the morning
with a slanting saffron strip
from the curtain to the divan.

It covered with a hot ochre
the neighbouring forest, the houses of the village,
my bed, the damp pillow
and the edge of the wall behind the book shelf.

I remembered why
the pillow was damp.
I dreamed that you came one after
the other through the forest to see me off.

You walked in a crowd, separately and in pairs,
suddenly somebody remembered that today
is the sixth of August Old Style,
the Transfiguration of the Lord.

Usually a light without a flame
comes out on that day from Mount Tabor,
and the autumn, clear as a sign,
rivets gazes to itself.

And you went through the thin, beggarly,
naked, trembling alder thicket
into the ginger-red cemetery copse
which glowed like a honey cake.

The imposing sky neighboured
the treetops that had fallen silent,
and the distance echoed and called with the long
drawn out voices of the cocks.

In the forest like a public land surveyor
death stood in the middle of the graveyard,
looking at my dead pale face
so as to dig a grave the right length.

Everyone physically sensed
a quiet voice close by.
It was my former prophetic voice
that resounded untouched by decay.

'Farewell, azure of the Transfiguration,
and gold of the second Salvation.
Soften with a woman's final caress
the bitterness of my fateful hour.

Farewell, years of hardship,
we will say farewell to the woman throwing
down a challenge to the abyss of humiliation!
I am your battlefield.

Farewell, spread out sweep of the wing,
free stubbornness of flight,
and the image of the world, presented in the word,
and creation, and miracle-working.'

15

Winter Night

Snow, snow over the whole land
across all boundaries.
The candle burned on the table,
the candle burned.

As in summer, swarms
of midges fly to a flame,
snowflakes fluttered
around the windowframe.

Blown snow stuck
rings and arrows on the glass.
The candle burned on the table,
the candle burned.

Shadows were lying
on the lighted ceiling,
of crossed arms, crossed legs,
crossed destinies.

Two shoes fell
noisily on the floor.
The night light wept
wax drops on a dress.

Everything was lost in
the greying white snow haze.
The candle burned on the table,
the candle burned.

Draught at the candle from the corner,
the heat of temptation
angel-like raised two wings
in the form of a cross.

Snow fell all February
and now and then
the candle burned on the table,
the candle burned.

16
Parting

A man looks from the threshold
not recognising his house.
Her leaving was like a flight,
everywhere havoc has left its mark.

Chaos everywhere in the rooms,
he doesn't notice the extent
of the destruction
because of his tears and the oncoming migraine.

A roaring in his ears since morning.
Is he conscious or dreaming?
And why does the thought of the sea
creep unceasingly into his mind?

When through the hoar frost on the window
God's world is not visible,
his inescapable anguish is doubly
like the waste of the sea.

She was so dear to him
in every feature,
like the shores that are close to the sea
with the whole line of surf.

Like the turmoil that floods
the reeds after a storm,
her features and figure
went down to the depth of his soul.

In the years of trial,
an unthinkable life,
she was washed up against him
in a wave of fate from the seabed.

Amid countless obstacles,
bypassing danger,
the wave carried her, carried her
and brought her to him in earnest.

And now, look, she has left,
forcibly perhaps.
Parting will eat into both of them,
anguish will gnaw their bones.

And the man looks round:
in the moment of her departure
she turned everything upside down
out of the drawers of the chest.

He wanders around and till darkness comes
he puts back in the drawers
the scattered scraps
and the patterns she had cut out.

And pricking himself
on a needle sticking out in the sewing
he suddenly sees all of her
and weeps silently.

20
A Miracle

He went from Bethane to Jerusalem,
already tormented by the sadness of forebodings.

Prickly bushes stood scorched on the steep slope,
over the nearby hut the smoke did not move,
the air was hot, and the reeds motionless,
the peace of the Dead Sea was immovable.

And in bitterness that contested the bitterness of the sea
he walked with a small crowd of clouds
along the dusty road to some house in the town,
walked to the city to a gathering of disciples.

And he was so deep in thought
that the field in dejection smelt of wormwood.
Everything fell quiet. He stood alone in the middle,
and the landscape lay flat on its back in oblivion.
Everything was mixed up: heat and desert,
and lizards and springs and brooks.

A fig-tree stood not far away,
completely without fruit, just branches and leaves.
And he said to it: 'Whom do you profit?
What joy do you bring me in your stupor?

'I thirst and hunger, and you are barren
and it is more joyless to meet you than granite.
O how offensive and ungifted you are!
Remain so till the end of time.'

A tremour of judgement ran through the tree,
like the spark of lightning on a lightning conductor,
and burnt the fig-tree to ash.

Had it found in that time a moment of freedom
for the leaves, the branches and the roots and the trunk,
the laws of nature might have intervened.
But a miracle is a miracle, and a miracle is God.
When we are in confusion, then amid the disorder
it overtakes us in a flash, unawares.

Magdalene I

Scarcely night and my demon is here beside me,
my retribution for the past.
The memories of debauchery
come and suck my heart,
when a slave of men's fancies
I was a devil-possessed evil woman
and the street was my shelter.

A few minutes are left
and the silence of the grave will come,
but before these come
my life overflowing the edge
like an alabaster vessel
I smash before you.

O where now would I be,
my Teacher and my Saviour
if at nights by the table
eternity did not wait for me
like a new visitor
seduced by me in the net of my trade.

But explain what sin means,
and death and hell and the sulphur flame,
when I, in front of everyone's eyes,
as a graft grows into a tree,
have grown into you in my boundless anguish.

When your feet, Jesus,
rest on my knees,
I am perhaps learning to embrace
the four-sided shaft of the cross,
and fainting, I strain against your body
preparing you for burial.

25
The Garden of Gethsemane

The bend of the road was lit indifferently
by the twinkling of distant stars.
The road went by the Mount of Olives,
below the hill flowed the Kedron.

The field of grass tailed off in the middle.
Beyond it the Milky Way started.
Grey-haired, silver olive trees
tried to step on air in the distance.

Someone's garden was at the end, an allotment.
Leaving the disciples outside,
he said to them: 'My soul is mortally grieved,
stay here and watch with me.'

He refused without hostility,
like a refusal of borrowed things,
omnipotence and miracle-working,
and he was now like mortals, like us.

The night's expanse now seemed the edge
of annihilation and non-being.
The space of the universe was uninhabited,
and the garden alone was a place for living in.

And looking into these black chasms,
empty, without beginning or end,
in a bloody sweat he prayed the Father
that this cup of death would pass by.

Having appeased his deathly exhaustion with prayer,
he went outside the fence. On the earth
the disciples overcome by sleep
sprawled on the roadside feather-grass.

He aroused them: 'The Lord granted you
to live in my days, and you lie here inert.
The hour of the Son of Man has struck.
He gives himself up into the hands of sinners.'

And he had just said this when out of the blue
came a crowd of slaves and a rabble of down-and-outs,
torches, swords, and in front Judas
with a traitor's kiss on his lips.

Peter resisted the ruffians with his sword
and cut off the ear of one man,
but he hears: 'The argument cannot be decided
by steel. Sheathe your sword, man.

Could not my Father send me here
thousands of winged legions?
And then, not touching a hair of my head,
the enemies would scatter without a trace.

But the book of life has come to the page
which is more precious than all sacred things.
Now what has been written must be fulfilled,
let it come about. Amen.

You see, the course of the centuries is like a parable
and may catch fire on the way.
In the name of its terrible majesty
I will go to the grave and voluntary torture.

I will go to the grave and on the third day rise again,
and as the rafts float down the river,
out of the darkness sail the centuries
like a string of barges to me for judgement.

OSIP MANDELSTAM 1891-1938

Sleeplessness. Homer. Taut sails.
I have read half the catalogue of ships:
that long brood, that train of cranes
that once rose over Greece.

Like a wedge of cranes to foreign boundaries —
on the heads of the kings the foam of the gods.
Where are you sailing to? Without Helen
what would Troy alone be to you, O Achaean men?

The sea and Homer — all is moved by love.
Which one should I listen to? And Homer falls silent
and the black sea roars rhetorically
and surges up to my pillow with a thundering crash.

Tristia

I have studied the science of parting
in night laments when a woman's hair flows loose.
The oxen chew, and waiting lingers on,
the last hour of city vigils,
and I honor the rite of that cockcrowing night,
when raising their burden of itinerant sorrow
cried out eyes looked into the distance,
and a woman's weeping mixed with the singing of the Muses.

Who can tell at the word parting
what separation awaits us?
What does the cock's exclamation augur,
when the fire burns on the acropolis,
and at the dawn of some new life,
when the ox chews lazily in the passage,
why the cock, the herald of the new life
flaps its wings on the city wall?

I love the custom of spinning:
the shuttle scurries to and fro, the spindle hums,
look, barefoot Delia flies
to meet you, like swan's down.
O the bare basis of our life,
how poor is the language of joy!
Everything happened a long time ago, everything will repeat itself again,
and only the moment of recognition for us is sweet.

So let it be: a little transparent figure
lies on a clear earthenware plate,
like a spread out squirrel skin,
leaning over the wax a girl looks,
not for us to tell fortunes about the Greek Erebus,
wax is for women as bronze is for men.
The lot falls on us only in battle,
to them it is given to die telling fortunes.

1918

As an equal with the others
I want to honor you,
from jealousy to cast spells
with my dry lips and mouth.
No words you say can moisten
my dried up thirsting lips,
the dense atmosphere is empty again
when I'm without you.

I am no longer jealous,
but I am wanting you,
and carry myself forward
as victim to be hung.
I never could have called you
either happiness or love,
to a wild alien essence
my blood's been subtly changed.

And just another moment
and I will say to you,
not happiness but torment
I always found in you.
Bitten in confusion,
your cherry tender lips
lead me on towards you
as criminal to crime.

Come back to me the sooner,
I'm frightened without you,
I never felt it stronger,
this hold you have on me,
and all I ever wanted
I now see clear as day,
I am no longer jealous,
but I am calling you.

   1920

How terrifying for the two of us is this life,
my largemouthed, comrade wife.

See how our Armenian tobacco crumbles,
little friend, simple one, cracking nuts for your birthday cake.

One could whistle life through like a starling
or eat it like a slice of hazel nut cake ...

But we both know that's impossible.

       October 1930 Tiflis

Don't talk to anyone,
forget all you saw —
a bird, an old woman, prison,
or anything more.

Or the shallow tremor of the fir trees
will come over you,
just as you open your lips
at the beginning of day.

You'll remember a wasp at the dacha,
a child's pencil box and inks,
or the bilberries in the forest
that you never picked.

       October 1930 Tiflis

For the thundering glory of future ages,
for the lofty generation of people,
I have deprived myself of the cup at the feast of the fathers,
of happiness and even my honour.

The wolf-hound age hurls itself on my shoulders,
but my blood is not the blood of a wolf,
rather stuff me like a Russian fur hat into the sleeve
of the hot overcoat of the Siberian steppes,

so as not to see the coward or the clinging mud,
or the bloodied bones on the rack,
so that all night through the blue polar foxes
should shine at me in their primaeval beauty.

Take me off into the night, where the Yenisey flows
and the pine tree reaches the stars,
because my blood is not the blood of a wolf,
and only an equal can kill me.

      17-28th March 1931

For Anna Akhmatova

Preserve my speech forever for its aftertaste of misfortune and smoke,
for the pitch of circular patience, for the shaming tar of work.
So the water of Novgorod wells ought to be black and sweet,
so that towards Christmas a star with seven fins should be reflected in it.

For this, my father, my friend and rough helper,
I, the unrecognised brother, black sheep of the people's family,
promise to build such dense frames
that the Tartars could lower the princes into the torture tubs.

If only they loved me, those frozen executioner's blocks!
The skittles bruise in the garden, their aim is to kill,
for this I will go my whole life through in a shirt of iron
and like Peter the Great find an axe in the woods for an execution.

    3rd May 1931 Khmelnitskaya

Octets

1

I love the appearance of cloth
when after two or three
and then four breaths
an extending sigh comes
and I feel so good and it's difficult for me
when the moment approaches —
and suddenly an arched stretching
sounds in my mumblings.

II

I love the appearance of cloth
when after two or three
and then four breaths
an extending sigh comes
and tracing open forms
with the arcs of sailing boats
space plays in half-sleep —
a child who never knew the cradle.

III

When you have destroyed all the rough drafts,
and hold steadfastly in your mind
a sentence without tedious footnotes
integral in its internal darkness,
and it holds itself up screwing up its eyes
on its own tension alone,
its reference to the paper was the same
as the cupola to the empty skies.

IV

Tell me, draughtsman of the desert,
geometer of the shifting sands,
surely the intractability of lines is not
more powerful than the blowing wind?
'The shudder of his Jewish worries
does not concern me.'
He moulds experience from a babbling
and drinks babbling from experience.

V

O butterfly, O Moslem woman,
all in a slit shroud,
lifeling and deathling,
such a big one this.
The biter with the large moustache
hid its head in a burnous.
O shroud unfurled like a flag —
fold your wings: I'm afraid.

VI

The notched paw of the maple
bathes in round corners,
and one can paint pictures on walls
from the colour flecks of butterflies.
There are mosques that are alive,
and now I have guessed it,
perhaps we are Hagia Sophia
with a numberless multitude of eyes.

VII

Schubert on the water and Mozart in the birds' chatter,
and Goethe, whistling on a twisting path,
and Hamlet, thinking in hurried footsteps,
took the pulse of the crowd and trusted in the crowd.
Perhaps the whisper was born before the lips,
and leaves circled and fell when there was no wood,
and those to whom we dedicate our experience
had acquired their features before that experience.

VIII

In needle sharp plague goblets
we drink the delusion of causes,
we touch with hooks magnitudes
small as an easy death.
Even where the spillikins had coupled together
a child conserves his silence —
the great universe sleeps in the cradle
of a little eternity.

IX

And I walk out from space
into the overgrown garden of magnitudes,
and pluck fleeting constancy
and self-consciousness of causes.
Infinity, I alone read
your herbal without anybody else,
a wild, leafless book of healing,
a huge-rooted book of riddles.

X

The hard blue eye pierced with nature's law,
having overcome its memorization,
the rocks play the fool in Christ in the earth's crust,
and a groan tears itself like ore from the chest,
and the deaf miscarriage stretches
like a road, curling into a horn,
to understand the inner plenty of space,
and the petal and the cupola's pledge.

XI

The minute appendage of sixth sense,
or the sincipital eye of the lizard,
the monasteries of snails and sea-shells,
the conversation of flickering eyelashes,
how close is the unobtainable!
You cannot untwine it, nor glance at it,
as though a note is placed in your hand
and you must answer it immediately.

May 1932-July 1935

Poem to the Unknown Soldier

Let this air be witness —
its long range heart —
and in dug outs active and omnivorous,
the ocean, windowless matter.

Why are these stars informers,
still they need to look on, for what?
In judgement of the judge and witness,
in the ocean, windowless matter.

Rain, the enemy sower, remembers
its anonymous manna,
how the forest of little crosses took aim,
the ocean and the wedge of war.

The cold sick people
will kill, hunger and be cold,
and in his famous grave
the unknown soldier is lain.

Teach me sickly swallow,
who has unlearned how to fly,
how I can keep control with this grave in the air,
without rudder and wing.

For Mihail Lermontov
I will render you a stern contract,
as the grave straightens out the hunchback
and the pit in the air attracts.

2

These worlds threaten us
with rustling grape clusters,
and they hang with stolen towns,
golden slips of the tongue and slanders —
berries of poisoned cold,
the tents of tensile constellations,
the golden worlds of constellations.

3

Through the decimal-meaning ether,
the transparent light of velocities ground
into a beam begins the count
with bright pain and a mole of nils,

and beyond the field of fields flies
a new field like a triangular crane —
the news flies on the bright dusty road
and is bright from yesterday's battle.

The news flies on the bright dusty road,
I am not Leipzig, I am not Waterloo,
I am not the Battle of the Peoples, I am something new,
from me the world will be bright.

In the depth of the blackmarbled oyster
the flamelet of Austerlitz has died,
the Mediterranean swallow screws up its eyes,
the plague sand of Egypt is sticky.

4

An Arabian mishmash and medley,
the light of velocities ground into a beam,
and with its slanting foothills
the beam stands on my retina.

Millions killed off cheaply
trampled the grass in the wilderness,
good night, all the best to them
on behalf of the earthwork fortresses.

The incorruptible trenched sky,
the sky of multiple trench deaths,
for you, from you all bought up
I rush towards you in the darkness with my lips.

Beyond the craters, the filled in holes and the scree
over which he made his slow hazy way,
the havoc maker, sullen and pockmarked
and humiliated genius of the graves.

5

The infantry die well,
and the night choir sings well,
over the flattened smile of Shweik,
and over the bird's spear of Don Quixote,
and over the knight's bird claw.
The cripple will be friends with man:
work will be found for both of them.
Along the outskirts of the age
a little family of wooden crutches knocks —
hey comradeship — the globe of the earth.

6

Is it for this that the skull must develop,
forehead entire — temple to temple —
so that into its precious eye sockets
the troops could do nothing but flow in.
The skull develops away from life,
forehead entire — temple to temple —
it teases itself with the cleanness of its sutures,
clarifies with a cupola of meaning,
foams with thought, dreams of itself —
the cup to the cup, homeland to the homeland,
the little cap sewn with a starry seam —
the little cap of happiness — Shakespeare's father.

7

The clarity of the ash and the vigilance of the sycamore
scarcely red rushes to their home,
as though starting to talk through fainting fits
both skies with their dull fire.

78

Allied to us is only the surplus,
ahead is not the downfall but the survey,
and to fight for the air we live on,
this glory is not an example to others.

My conscience speaks out
in its half-fainting existence,
do I drink this broth without choice,
and eat my own head under the fire?

Is the package of fascination
prepared in the empty space
so that the white stars scarcely red
should rush back to their home?

Do you hear, step mother of the starry camp —
night, what will happen now and after?

8

Aortas are flooded with blood
and a whisper runs through the ranks:
'I was born in ninety four,
I was born in ninety two ...'
And squeezing my worn out year of birth
into my fist, herded with the herd,
I whisper with bloodless mouth:
'I was born in the night of the second to the third
of January in the hopeless year
ninety two, and the centuries
surround me with fire.'

1937 Voronezh

BULAT OKUDZHAVA 1924-

Francois Villon

While the world is still turning, while it is full of light,
give O Lord to each man what he is without:
give a head to the wise, to the coward a horse for flight,
give to the happy money,
                    and don't forget about me.

While the world is still turning, Lord all's in your power,
flood the power greedy people with power up to their throats,
give to the generous breathing — deep till the day burns low,
give forgiveness to Cain,
                    and don't forget about me.

I know you can do everything, I believe in the wisdom in you,
as the soldier shot dead that he will live in heaven,
as every hearer believes the calmness of your words too,
and we believe unconsciously in the power we are given.

O Lord, green-eyed God of mine,
while the world is still turning, not knowing what it's all about,
while world's time and fire remain,
in giving a little to all,
                    don't forget about me.

Ballad of my love, my life

And like the first love — it burns the heart,
and the second love — it clings to the first,
but the third love —
a key trembles in the lock,
a key trembles in the lock,
you hold a box.

And like the first fight is no one's fault,
and the second fight is anyone's fault,
but the third fight
is just my fault
and my fault
by all is caught.

And like the first deceit is a sultry sunset,
and the second deceit is a drunken feast,
but the third deceit
is blacker than the night,
is blacker than the night,
terror of the fight.

Ballad of the Paper Soldier

A soldier lived upon this earth,
handsome he grew bolder,
but he was a child's toy from birth,
he was a paper soldier.

The world it wanted changing —
happiness to his order,
but he hung on a puppet string,
he was a paper soldier.

He would be happy in fire and smoke
to die for you twice over,
but you fussed over him and spoke:
'You are a paper soldier.'

He cursed his worldly fate
not thirsting for the quiet life
and begged and begged for the fiery state
forgot his paper life.

The fire? Well go, well off you go,
and he walked off the bolder,
and then he burnt in a puff and blow,
he was a paper soldier.

Ballad of the Soldiers' Boots

You hear the heavy tread of boots,
and the birds go crazy, fly about,
and the women look and wring their hands,
where they look you understand.

You hear the heavy thunder of drums,
soldier say goodbye to her, her to him,
the platoon goes off into the mist, the mist, the mist,
and the past is just a kiss, a kiss, a kiss.

And where soldier boy is our courage,
when we return back from war's rage?
I suppose that it will be stolen by the women
and held like a fledgeling to the skin.

And where are our women, my friend,
when we come through the door at road's end?
They'll meet us and take us in the house,
but raped and robbed the atmosphere chokes us.

And we curse the past and Christ,
look to the future with hope and light,
but in the fields the crows grow fatter,
and on our heels the war's heavy thunder.

And again round the corner tread of boots,
and the birds go crazy, fly about,
and the women look and wring their hands,
as marches off another soldier band.

ANDREI VOZNESENSKY 1933-

Troubadours and Burghers

Let's face it, our cause is long lost:
you've walked on our corpses.

— but though you've survived and destroyed us
you were always the corpses, while we were the trumpets.

The Trumpet of Fate
cried out in the teeth
of history's dumbness
with the chill of the Gods.
You were the cowards, we the trumpets.

You built up walls around us
because we had your women
in ecstasies
— we burst through the thick walls
and sound the trumpets still ...

We're the troubadours with the fool's touch:
how right you were to trample on us
to take over every inch of property ...
You own Space
but Time flies with us.

Do you admit to yourselves
in your safe soundproofed mansions
that you envy the trumpet?
Corpses — live again! Trumpets — cry on!

Translated with the assistance
of Michael Horovitz and Andrei Voznesensky

Applefall

I visited the artist after death
accompanied by the local she-devil.
His rooms were empty as frames without pictures;
but the sound of Tchaikovsky came from one of them.

I walked through the deserted halls
with my tall Afro-haired guest;
it was like holding onto a black balloon.

Behind a door, in an armchair,
sat a thought in the form of a woman
surrounded by forty portraits.
The thought hit me — like a creative impulse —
signalling; 'Don't interrupt.'

What a strain to be an artist's model!
Three-legged easels laboured over her.
I sensed loneliness
in their swirling, ever changing structures —

here a nail, there three eyes, a captured bayonet
— how he must have loved her then!
No fulfilment
for the creative impulse.

Above the radiator Tchaikovsky
revolved under Gennady Rozhdestvensky's
baton. My Afro-balloon pleaded
to be loosed to the winds. A thunderstorm
crashed in the sky. Clouds exuded the scent
of apple sacks.

Everyone was feeling it now
— as though the place was being aired:
the impulse preceding creation,
the passion preceding creation,
the sorrow preceding creation
rocked the buildings and the trees!

Apples fell. The strings
and boughs were weeping:
so many apples, you could shovel them up!
On my knees I gathered them,
these fallen apples of the applefall.
I threw off my shirt: like cold fists
they bastinadoed my naked shoulderblades.
I guffawed under the applefall;
there was no apple tree
— just apples falling.
I tied the sleeves of my chastened shirt
and stuffed it full of fruit like a basket,
How heavy it weighed, and trembling, redolent —
I gasped —
a woman was sat there, in a man's shirt. . . .
I had created you from fallen apples —
out of dust — my marvellous one, my waif!
Under your sideways-slanting eye was stuck
a birthmark like a tiny dark grain.
I'd played co-author to creation.
That's how we make snowmen in the yard
from snow-apples, on our knees
— that's how we make our lovers.
I introduced you as a guest to the lady of the house.
You handed your Eve's apples out to all the guests
and earthed them with your black jive-talk.

Who would have guessed that you, smiling there
in a shirt like a mini-dress
would forget yourself, fall in love, throw off your shirt
and roll on the ground like balls of quicksilver.

91

Above the bus stop a cloud
smelled of winter apple sacks.
The black balloon flew off. Wind swept over the world.
Farewell, spontaneous creation!

Had you spent the night in the creator's dacha
cold and alone, on prickly sackcloth?
— These words came to you:
'Thank you for your giving. Much thanks, creator
that I was able to be part of you,
part of the sea and dry land, of Tsvetayeva's garden
— thanks for granting me all this:
that I haven't lived my life like a mouse in a hole,
that I haven't double-dealt with you, Time,
even when you gave me two fingers —
and thanks for these frenzied blows
— for my putting pen to paper, even,
and for this poem;
and though you'll snuff it tomorrow
I thank you for giving me
the short sweet apples of her knees —
for the geniality of your models,
the unnameable uniqueness of your ideas ...'

And already dreaming, repeated:
'I worship you for your gifts.'

Night gates opened into the world.
You went away. Dogs howled.
It's no good visiting the artist when he's dead

— do it while you're still alive.

Translated with assistance from Mara Amats
Michael Horovitz and Andrei Voznesensky

YEVGENY YEVTUSHENKO 1933-

Deep Snow

I am skiing over the white snow,
skiing and thinking,
                        what can I do in this life?
I look at myself,
                strain,
                        and memories come back.
What do I know?
                        I know nothing.
I am skiing over the white snow.
Nogin Square is in a beautiful town.
I can see it from here.
A certain girl lives there.
                        She's
not a wife to me.
                        She's not in love with me.
Who's to blame?
                        Ah, the white fluttering snow.
I'm skiing.
                I feel anxious and light-headed at the same time
Deep snow.
                        Deep breathing.
Overhead it's also deep.
I have to go far.
Creak, dear skis,
                        creak,
and you,
            my distant one,
                        forget your troubles.
Take heart.
                        Buy yourself something new,
Sleep peacefully,
                        I won't get lost.
I want to smoke,
                matches break.

95

I'm tired of skiing away from myself.
I go home,
            In the hot train carriage
my skis will get in someone's way.
I arrive at a certain girl's.
                        She'll stop what she's doing.
She wears her hair in plaits in a garland.
She missed me from afar.
She'll ask to be kissed.
'Did the skis get in the way?'
                        she quietly asks.
'No, no' I answer, 'there was no trouble at all.'
And I think to myself:
                    'Would you like some tea, my dear?'
'No'
    'What's with you today — I can't understand it,
Where are you?'
                    I shake my head.
What can I answer?
                    Then I say:
'I'm skiing over the white snow.'

1955

The Cocks

To T. Chiladze

The cocks are crowing by the sea,
clashing their wings over the Crimea.
They crow, and their crowing
shakes the ceilings of the dachas.
They exhort us to be loud and flourish,
and with this aim in mind they wake us,
they call for the future
and bless the present.

What is my present, what is my future?
I don't know this in detail,
but there is one thing I hold no mystery
at the beginning of the day and at its close.
Among the trivial tortures and caresses,
you, the chief caresser and torturer,
my tormented Muse,
with dark rings under your eyes.
Am I loved by you? Loved I am,
but somehow with bitterness and sadness.
You look at me as though to say farewell,
as though I've become someone alien.

Unloving I betray you,
with mere likenesses of your self.
I ascribe your name
to those who are nothing like you.
But feeling the pain of this lie
you wait for me like a young girl
clasping your little knees,
without loud tears, without reproaches.

How can I turn your 'farewell'
into a simple 'hello' in the morning.
Don't be shy; be strong,
and make demands, don't plead.
Although my betrayals cannot be numbered,
and I'm judged with a crooked smile,
for me you are the future,
and for me you are the present.

The cocks are crowing by the sea,
summoning us to get up and get dressed.
They call us not to give up,
leaving giving up to the cowards.
They call us to burst our sleep,
whether its the sleepiness of our conscience
or the sleepiness of reason and our arms.

Thank you life for the laborious labour,
for your stubborn cocks.
Wherever I hide myself
they will find me, will find me.
Thank you for the dreams,
thank you for the awakenings,
for the bitter premonitions
that you gave to me.
For the multitude of my sins
and for your sinlessness,
for the sea and its boundlessness,
and once more, for the cocks.

     1960
     Koktebel

For V. Aksyonov

I am like a train,
                  that has been rushing so many years
between Yes city,
                  and No city.
My nerves are taut
                  as wires,
between No city
                  and Yes city.

All is dead and terrified in No city.
It is like a study upholstered with sadness.
In it every object frowns in on itself.
In it every portrait looks out suspiciously.
In it in the mornings they wipe the floors with bile.
In it the divans are false, in it the walls are built of troubles.
Like Hell there will you get good advice,
or, let's say, a bunch of flowers, or simply a greeting.
The typewriters chatter out copies of their answer:
'No-no-no ... no-no-no ... no-no-no ...'
And when the light has died down completely
in it the ghosts start their gloomy ballet.
And getting a ticket to get away
from black No city is a hell of a task ...

But in Yes city life is like a thrush's song.
This city is without walls, it's like a nest.
Any star in the sky begs to be embraced,
any lips beg for yours without shame,
whispering scarcely audibly: 'Everything's nonsense!'
The mignonette teasingly begs to be plucked,
and lowing the flock offer up milk,
and there is no trace of suspicion,
and wherever you want to go momentarily
trains, boats and planes take you there,

and burbling as years the water scarce babbles
'Yes-yes-yes … yes-yes-yes … yes-yes-yes …'
Only sometimes, to be honest, it bores me
that so much is given me almost without effort,
in the multicoloured shining Yes city …

Better for me to rush for the rest of my days
between Yes city
                    and No city!
Let the nerves be taut as wires
between No city
                    and Yes city!

LEONID ARANZON 1939-1970

In the hours of sleeplessness I love to sleep in a chair,
and see a dream unsplittable from those pictures I see when wide awake
and waking to see the dream again.

An old writing desk, a candle, a bed,
and doors behind which lies in an empty coffin
the Old Maid of Spades,
I go up to her to kiss her on the forehead.

Time creates a half-fragmentation,
a garden forgotten by someone languishes in the corner,
tormenting consciousness a spider drops.

My wife's face is turned to the South,
and all is in sadness which no longer exists.

        *   *   *

Alas, I'm alive. Deadly dead.
Words were filled with silence.
The gift rug of nature
I rolled up into a primordial roll.

Before everything that exists I lie
at nights, looking at them intently.
Glen Gould, the pianist of my fate
plays with noted signs.

Here is comfort in sadness,
but its result is even more terrible.
Thoughts rush not meeting.

Airy flower, without roots,
here is the butterfly on my hand,
look, life is given, what can one do with it?

To Al. Al.

Horatio, Pylades, Altshuler, brother,
my sister, Ophelia, Juliet,
who playing the masquerade for so many years
is dressed as the gloomy Altshuler.

O,o, my Altshuler, I hope that with this
I too am Horatio, your Altshuler, Pylades,
and I am your sister, dressed up in the outfit
of the composer of such a long sonnet.

Look here — here there is nothing at all!
My friend, my brother Ophelia, it's easy to make fun of you.
My neuter Horatio, you are living flattery to all,

but don't be embarrassed: I'm not joking with you —
where there is nothing at all, there is something else,
a sacred nothing is there which never diminishes.

Empty Sonnet

Who loved you more passionately than I?
May God preserve you, God preserve you, O God preserve you.
The gardens stand, the gardens stand, stand in the night.
And you in the gardens, and you in the gardens standing too.

I would like to, I would like to instil my sadness
into you, instil it so as not to alarm
your sight of the night grass, your sight of its stream,
so that that sadness, so that that grass became our bed.

To pierce into the night, to pierce into the garden, to pierce into you,
to lift eyes, to lift eyes to compare the night in the garden
with the heavens, and the garden in the night, and the garden
which is full of your night voices.

I go towards them. Face full of eyes,
so that you could stand in them, the gardens stand.

     1969

It's somehow sad in Petersburg.
You gaze at the sky and can't find it.
Only the dead carcass of summer
is a guest in my empty lorgnette.
I half lie. I half fly.
Who is half flying to meet me?
We fly, nodding in parting,
one to the other into the parted lips.
No, not even an angel
can write with pen at such a time:
'The trees are locked up and bolted,
but from where is this rustle of leaves of leaves?'

For Rita

I even fell out of love with nature,
the lakes dark with forests,
the hindquarters of beautiful mares,
which I looked at for hours.

And that sadness itself lies heavily on me,
the landscape decorated with Danaea,
or the fat bee at midday
flying to the fields for its tax;

all this, not brightening my thoughts,
just irritates, bores me to death,
and the gardens riotously thick
with August don't involve me.

     1966

Will someone really dare to embrace you?
Night and the river in the night are not so beautiful:
O how could you dare to be so beautiful,
that having lived my life, I want to live again?

I am Caesar. But you are so noble
that I am in the crowd, staring respectfully,
here are your breasts! Here are her legs, the same,
and if her visage is like this, what a wonder her womanhood is!

If you were to be a night butterfly
I would be a candle flying before you.
The night sparkles with river and skies.

I look at you — so silent before me.
I would like to touch you with my hand
to retain a long memory.

      1969 Summer

Swan

A girl sat round me,
and facing her and with my back to her
I stood leaning on a tree,
and the carp swam to the watering hole.

The carp swam, a maquette of the sunset,
the cockchafer of the swampy waters,
and the water-lily leaf closed the entrance
with a green patch.

The swan was a vessel of the morning,
brother to the white flowers,
it rocked here and there.

Like a bowstring, sharply
its breast bent:
it was a nightingale with no warble.

1965

Along the walls by the wards,
candle-lit by the moon,
the rustleless garden of shadows
opened out before me.

Leafless garden of shadows,
the garden on the other side,
was snatched away
from the windows of hospitals.

When the lights were put out,
there, in the darkness of the wards
on a lustreless wall
the garden began to surface.

Garden burst out, like sweat,
through whiteness of wall,
a graveyard,
the long light of the moon.

The soundless garden in the dark
was as hazy
as a blurred negative
alone in the depth of the wards.

April fevered the bushes,
and in pauses between dreams
the garden hung
like a tapestry against windows and doors.

As though separating from dreams
I saw through them
behind the brick of the wall
the buzzing of a living double.

Alone to all cripples,
alone to the darkness of the wards,
multiple as a track,
the garden on the other side.

Water in the gardens, gardens standing in water.
Peaceful walks beside them.
The empty castles of Petersburg,
and the one-starred sky.
Everything is beautiful. Sadness is everywhere.
I wander unrecognised
in this created nature,
like a bearded Pushkin.

Poem Written in Expectation of Awakening

The fauna frolic in the flora,
trampling and eating it.
Danae sits on a hill,
her eyes misted over.
There is sadness all around
because the young girl is
fornicating with the hill.

*   *   *

With a scented eruption in the spreading lava of flowers
the hill is flooded, and to break off the coming bliss is not in one's power.
From every pore springs beat, springs of flowers and the glory of God,
and the symbol of a butterfly flies up as the expiration of the lava
    steam-cloud.

Two Identical Sonnets

I

My love, sleep, my little golden one,
dressed all in satin skin.
I seem to think we've met somewhere:
I know your nipple so well and your underwear.

How it suits you, how it goes with you, it's just you,
all this day, all this Bach, all this body.
This day, and this Bach and this plane
flying there, flying here, flying somewhere.

Into this garden, into this Bach, into this moment,
fall asleep, my love, fall asleep without covering up:
countenance and bottom, bottom and womanhood, womanhood and
    countenance,
let all sleep, let all sleep, my living one.
Not approaching one iota, not one step,
give yourself up to me in all gardens and declensions.

II

My love, sleep, my little golden one,
dressed all in satin skin.
I seem to think we've met somewhere:
I know your nipple so well and your underwear.

How it suits you, how it goes with you, it's just you,
all this day, all this Bach, all this body.
This day, and this Bach and this plane
flying there, flying here, flying somewhere.

Into this garden, into this Bach, into this moment,
fall asleep, my love, fall asleep without covering up:
countenance and bottom, bottom and womanhood, womanhood and
    countenance,
let all sleep, let all sleep, my living one.
Not approaching one iota, not one step,
give yourself up to me in all gardens and declensions.

How good it is in these abandoned places,
abandoned by men but not the gods.
It's raining, sodden the beauty
of the ancient mountain forest.

It's raining, sodden the beauty
of the ancient mountain forest.
We're alone here. No people are our equals.
Oh, how blessed it is to drink in the mist.

We're alone here. No people are our equals.
Oh, how blessed it is to drink in the mist.
Let us remember the path of the fallen leaf,
and the idea that we go on after us.

Let us remember the path of the fallen leaf,
and the idea that we go on after us.
Who rewarded us with these dreams,
or did we give ourselves this reward?

Who rewarded us with these dreams,
or did we give ourselves this reward?
To shoot oneself here one needs no devil:
no burden in the soul, or powder in the gun.

Not even a gun. God sees that
to shoot oneself here one needs nothing.

ILYA BOKSTEIN 1937–

In Memory of Leonid Aranzon

Here apart from the silence
there's someone missing,
someone missing.
Only surprise remains.
The rain streams down,
as a quiet thin light.
A sodden leaf.
A green eclipse.
A sodden leaf.
A hint of freedom.
The break: now no people are our equals.
Now we're a little swayed by the wind,
although there is no wind. There is the purity of the leaf.
Here apart from the silence there is no poet.
The surprise of sodden leaves.
The rain streams down so quietly as though it were light,
as though it were the secret of its freedom.
He realised: no parabellum is necessary here,
no darkness in the soul, not even light sadness,
and happiness isn't even worth
a bird's tailfeathers.
To melt in time with the silence.
Beauty is sodden,
and the drops are heavy,
as freshness delicately white,
and the drops are heavy,
as freshness — a white joke.
I don't remember whether autumn or spring
fell with the rain.
Let us remember the path
of the fallen leaf.

The Evangelist John in the Wilderness

I read the Gospel to the sheep and the lions,
the grass and the stars,
to all who will undertake to rework
the world's consciousness,
so that they could have the chance to remember
that they listened to God
while they were still infants.

Job

Why do you argue with Satan over my soul?
So that you can create a book about it?
I shall avenge you with double
the misfortune that rained down on you,
so that you should love me not just for the good,
but in doubt of the most sacred things,
so that your doubting should not serve Satan.

Poem of Resurrection

On the road I forgot about fate,
and did not wait for my death.
I found, believe it or not,
a covenant thrown by the wayside.
I read in it the end to parting.
An evening poppy flowered by the path,
opening three petals like wings.
Where the petals narrowed it outlined
the wings of the Trinity in its oval crown,
the three faces of the universe.

        *   *   *

I saw God face to face,
peace glimmers in the mind.
Death senses
the blows of laughter.
The fragile tree of dreams
crumbles quietly.
What nature warmed
my ashes with a drop of conscience?
To caress that frail Body
and think of distant worlds.
I look at you from my nothingness,
as though born on a whim,
as though creation grants me
a special key,
and enlightenment floods my life.
Peace glimmers in the mind,
in my senses the fragile twig of dreams
trembles from destruction's laughter.

* * *

The light fades, shading the window,
outside it's also dark.
The silence of blackness is the obituary of Hell.
My room is filled with unclean spirits.
I wouldn't say they were evil, just unwelcome.
The hand of the Lord and the cross of the Master
light up on the ceiling.

HENRI VOLOKHONSKY 1936-

Maple

A maple appeared to me once in autumn
before sunset in the cold sky.
Its slender trunk black and frail
in the eastern quarter against the sun.
The yellow colour of the leaf was perfect
as though gold on its black twigs,
a transformation repeated twice on each branch
like stark decoration — and each
of the leaves forming the golden chamber
was endowed with such an obvious form
that their fallen shadows reminded me
of the archetype of autumn melancholy
on the recently swept earth
pressing into living projections
their individuality, not changing colour.
I only saw when I lifted my eyes again
the motionless steam of minted foliage,
bordered by serrated teeth, the rare globe
seemed to be a vessel with branches
filled with a few leaves.
And the maple, like a faintly glimmering vase
dropped its leaves one by one,
and I saw before me the symbol
of pre-dream euphoria and cool days.

Rainbow

At the last beat of rains transparent and sad
an insupportable first sign of a sparkle
on the clouds unseen by winds
fell and scattered, a wedding waving,
an apparition in the sky of wet grass
among the beautiful grasses,
the unexpected entered.
In the air, white and flowering with the pen
to cut out for the eye everything destructive,
stripped naked by a violet rib,
the green-grey dove beaten with blue
as two cold streams flowing towards the sea
chased and soared higher
and infused with golden crystals
the stretched horn both fiery and ruddy
as though a cornet ringing with heat and ash
and it was strung
and the branch over it was crimson
and its edge was crimson and so deep
it scarcely glimmered hardly dissolving in the air —
a blind knot of varied ribbons. . . .
And rearing the windblown form
of impossible brilliance to the eye
flowering over the waves slowly
the arc woven for the eyes delight.
Wished for and coloured
a light arm jutted through emptiness
flowing into the bordering ice
and the stones of the mountains embroidered in smoke.

I know, bird, where your cliff is.
You reared a flower in this distant current,
there where the cupola is high in the wind's rage,
the city of my dearest dream and sadness . . .

126

Prayer of Saint Francis

Spare me
Spare me from the spectacle of the empty edge of that cup in
    which there is no coin of Your mercy

Now
Now when rags around fall darkly
released from the brightness of standards
the moment of closed eyelids
this must be the best the finest moment
O if only I saw unblinking
the flower pond of Your glory
and the lake with a dear stream of forget-me-nots
The torrent
rolling up the chain, now thunders
The blacksmith with the star-counter
and these stand around here fearing, trembling as though waiting
    for news

Now the hour of silent closed lips
must be the complete hour of silently closed lips ...
O if only my breath
could melt the golden wax among the flowers
I would fly with them
over the stars like a slapping sail
and long and tortuously the honey flowed like rain
into these sticky fields
Then the earth would become a wine glass in the outstretched
    hand
But what silver did you put in so that it burned in a tight circle?
What fish did you throw into the fat for the sake of the beggar's
    torture?

You, it's You
But, tell us, how did You give back the sacred shoot, the wooden
    bridge on the shore of Your closeness?
Here, spare me.

127

The Summit of Mt. Hermon

A winged sun stands on the rock face,
sea in mist, sky in haze —
before them, Mt. Hermon's golden summit
sparkles in flight.

Hermon's summit glistens like a bull,
sides, clods and rocky humped hills,
head like a crown,
the golden summit of Mt. Hermon.

Ishtar disappears on the ship of the sunsetting rays,
Kinaret is in fog, Khula in haze,
standing as the guardian of the valley,
Mt. Hermon's golden summit.

The dove-blue summit of Vasan Mountain,
above which the sunset eagles
fly over ice packs
over the cold sky in flocks.

The double-headed sun stands on the rock face,
Hermon over Lebanon like a stone lion,
from the rock flows a caravan,
the golden river of Jordan.

Chamoix trumpet on dove-blue horns,
the hand of the sky, winged, golden,
high on the strings of the throne on
high, soars from Mt. Hermon.

Hermon is crowned with an eagle's head,
Jordan is crowned with a lion's head,
Vasan is an ox held in a spell,
crowned with the head of a bull.

Winged Hermon before them, the Cherubim
fly in grand wondering,
in the shining of the day's starriness,
over them in plumed abyss.

                *   *   *

Every time into our picture of the world
we mistakenly inscribe the spirit.
A star's eye sparkles in the sky,
the little ear pricks and flickers.
But, my dear one, why this strangeness,
to give to the aforesaid soul this acceptance
and create a god from its troubled dream?
The tired Creator who had long since ordered his creation scheme
transferred to art: the fate of ageing,
His order now has become as old and grand
as the very foundations He's laid on sand.
We only dare the juice to hand
of a twilight pumpkin to shattered feelings,
so that drinking the impossible bitterness
Eve should pant, the serpent hiss.

                *   *   *

Stilled the nightingale's dove in leaden sun rays
little dove-nightingale — dive, dive into deep water
float there as the mist into nowhere
past dove-blue sirens feathered with time-honoured face.

Let the gong shriek and the reed pipe gurgle with laughter-
white mica — on the bottom of the stream in quiet farewell
empty memory will not remember it in evil
or stamp it in silver thereafter.

White lotus, puffed roots, into which
the bagpipes of memory bit and encroached themselves:
the wicked tournament versus a person without speech.

Dancing crazily with the half-vocalised past, a drawn match
will not lead us into temptation. No one's nightingale preached.
Gloria in Excelsis wells up in leaden throats.

Allow me the wildness to sing wilfully of eternity
in the green spheres with the light rustle of a whistle,
brushing mute lips and then ringing,
a reed pipe on the strings of the idiot harpist.

The hoopoe soars — let the bronze sledgehammer,
and seers of sister go off and whisper,
but this is just the vengeance of death's passionate clamour,
that the reed of love implants as the gift of the artist.

Allow me to sing out, dear blindness,
my apology to you, dry flute.
The snow of light falls, a winged heel

has smashed the ice over the green trees of song,
of empty fate — over the sky of new fledglings,
and the spinners in terror needle-shuffle over the spokes' ashes.

Horse

Raven horse
Raven raven raved the horse
Horse raven wild raven
Whose raven's raving hubbub
Vanished wrenched
Neck's howl hovering soaring high
Heaving into sight, hurrah
Soaring again clutched by mane's disk
His head's ringing obelisk
Crown-bearing skull in thundering prism
Bearing the hoarse raven's long visage and voice
Wild raven rejoicing through lightning-bearing darkness
His panting and the cawing of the horse.